FOOD LOVERS

LUNCH

Food Lovers

LUNCH

RECIPES SELECTED BY JONNIE LÉGER

Trans
Atlantic
Press

All recipes serve four people, unless otherwise indicated.

For best results when cooking the recipes in this book, buy fresh ingredients and follow the instructions carefully. Make sure that everything is properly cooked through before serving, particularly any meat and shellfish, and note that as a general rule vulnerable groups such as the very young, elderly people, pregnant women, convalescents and anyone suffering from an illness should avoid dishes that contain raw or lightly cooked eggs.

For all recipes, quantities are given in standard U.S. cups and imperial measures, followed by the metric equivalent. Follow one set or the other, but not a mixture of both because conversions may not be exact. Standard spoon and cup measurements are level and are based on the following:

1 tsp. = 5 ml, 1 tbsp. = 15 ml, 1 cup = 250 ml / 8 fl oz.

Note that Australian standard tablespoons are 20 ml, so Australian readers should use 3 tsp. in place of 1 tbsp. when measuring small quantities.

The electric oven temperatures in this book are given for conventional ovens with top and bottom heat. When using a fan oven, the temperature should be decreased by about 20–40ºF / 10–20ºC – check the oven manufacturer's instruction book for further guidance. The cooking times given should be used as an approximate guideline only.

CONTENTS

SPICY SWEET POTATO SOUP WITH GINGER

Ingredients

2 orange colored sweet potatoes, peeled and cubed

2 onions, finely chopped

1 clove garlic, finely chopped

A ½ inch / 1 cm piece fresh ginger, finely chopped

2 tbsp. olive oil

2 tbsp. sherry vinegar

4 cups / 1 liter vegetable broth (stock)

½ cup / 100 ml whipping cream

Salt & pepper

1 pinch cinnamon

¾ cup / 75 g goat cheese

Cress, to garnish

Method

Prep and cook time: 30 min

1 Heat the oil in a saucepan and sauté the prepared ingredients. Now pour in the vinegar and the vegetable broth (stock), cover with a lid and simmer for about 15 minutes until the sweet potatoes are soft.

2 Purée the soup with a hand blender and mix in the cream and a little vegetable broth until the soup has the desired consistancy. Bring to a boil again and season with salt, pepper, and cinnamon.

3 Ladle the soup into bowls, crumble some goat cheese over the top, garnish with cress and serve.

SPINACH AND TOMATO QUICHE WITH PINE NUTS

Ingredients

For the pastry:

2¼ tsp / 10 g active dry yeast

1 pinch sugar

2 cups / 200 g all-purpose (plain) flour

½ cup / 250 ml lukewarm water

2 tbsp olive oil

½ tsp salt

For the filling:

2 tbsp vegetable oil

1 shallot, finely chopped

10 oz / 300 g frozen chopped spinach, thawed and squeezed dry

Zest of ½ lemon

1 cup / 150 g diced cooked ham

About 4 oz / 100 g sheep's cheese or Feta cheese, crumbled

¼ cup / 30 g pine nuts, toasted

5 eggs

Salt and freshly ground pepper, to taste

5 oz / 150 g cherry tomatoes, sliced

Basil leaves, to garnish

Pine nuts, to garnish

Method

Prep and cook time: 1 h plus 1 h 30 min rising time

1 Preheat the oven to 400°F (200°C / Gas Mark 6) Grease a 9-inch / 24 cm quiche dish.

2 For the pastry, mix the yeast with the sugar and two tablespoons lukewarm water in a small bowl. Mix in 2 tablespoons of the flour. Put the rest of the flour into a bowl and make a well in the center. Trickle the yeast mixture into the well, dust lightly with flour, cover and put in a warm place for 30 minutes to allow the yeast to start working.

3 Add the lukewarm water, oil and salt to the flour and gradually knead to a smooth dough. Knead well, then put back into the bowl. Cover with a cloth and put in a warm place for an hour or until doubled in volume.

4 For the filling, heat the oil in a skillet, add the shallot and sauté until soft. Add the spinach and lemon zest; cook gently for 2-4 minutes. Let cool and pour off any liquid. Mix the ham, cheese and pine nuts with the spinach. Lightly beat the eggs and blend into the spinach mixture. Season with salt and pepper and set aside.

5 Knead the dough for a couple of minutes and roll out thinly on a floured work surface. Line the quiche dish with the dough, pressing it onto the sides of the dish to form a rim. Turn the spinach mixture into the dish and arrange the tomatoes on top, pressing them in slightly. Bake for 25 to 30 minutes. Garnish with basil leaves and pine nuts and serve.

NOODLE SOUP WITH CHICKEN AND NUTS

Ingredients

4 cups / 1 liter vegetable broth (stock)

1 stick lemongrass

4 tbsp. light soy sauce

3 tbsp. lime juice

½ inch / 1 cm ginger, chopped

1 clove garlic, chopped

8 oz / 250 g chicken breast

1 red chili

1 cup / 120 g snow peas (mangetout)

2 tomatoes

2 Chinese cabbage leaves

7oz / 200 g Asian egg noodles

¾ cup / 40 g walnuts, roughly chopped

1 bunch fresh cilantro (coriander)

Method

Prep and cook time: 25 min

1 Put the vegetable broth (stock), lemongrass, two tablespoons of soy sauce, two tablespoons of lime juice, the ginger and garlic in a saucepan and bring to a boil. Now add the chicken breast, cover with a lid and simmer for about 15 minutes over a low to medium heat.

2 Wash the chili and cut into rings. Add to the broth. Wash the snow peas (mangetout); wash and deseed the tomatoes. Clean the Chinese cabbage leaves. Cut the vegetables into thin strips.

3 Remove the lemon grass and the chicken breast from the broth. Cut the meat into bite-size pieces.

4 Put the Asian noodles in the soup and simmer for about 2 minutes in the broth. Add the vegetables and the meat and warm. Season with soy sauce and lime juice. Garnish with the roughly chopped walnuts and cilantro (coriander) leaves before serving.

PEPPERS WITH SPINACH AND MONKFISH STUFFING

Ingredients

4 red bell peppers

2 cups / 400 g rice

½ lb / 250 g monkfish, cut into bite-size chunks

2 tbsp olive oil

2 shallots, finely chopped

2 cloves garlic, minced

About 3 cups /100 g spinach leaves

1 bunch basil, leaves separated and chopped (reserve a few leaves for garnish)

½ bunch parsley, chopped

Salt and freshly ground pepper, to taste

Scant 1 cup / 200 ml vegetable broth (stock), divided

3 egg yolks

Method

Prep and cook time: 50 min

1 Preheat the oven to 350°F (180°C / Gas Mark 4).

2 Blanch the bell peppers: slice off the top third of each to make a lid and remove the cores. Fill a large bowl with ice water. Bring a large saucepan of salted water to a boil. Add the peppers and their lids; cook 8-10 minutes; quickly remove them with a slotted spoon to the ice water to cool. Drain.

3 Meanwhile, cook the rice according to the package instructions; keep warm.

4 Heat the oil in a skillet; add the shallots and garlic and sauté until translucent. Add the spinach, basil and parsley and cook until the spinach wilts. Then mix in the monkfish, season with salt and pepper and remove from the heat. Drain in a sieve and squeeze lightly, reserving the liquid. Stuff the bell peppers with the fish and spinach stuffing, put on the lids and stand upright in a baking dish. Add half of the vegetable broth (stock) and bake for about 15 minutes, until cooked through.

5 Meanwhile beat the spinach liquid with the rest of the broth and the egg yolks over a bowl of hot water until light and foamy. Season to taste with salt and pepper.

6 Put the stuffed bell peppers on warmed plates, add rice and herb foam and serve garnished with basil.

ASPARAGUS RISOTTO

Ingredients

1 lb / 500 g asparagus, trimmed

1 pinch sugar

Salt, to taste

2 tbsp butter, divided

1 shallot, finely diced

2 cups / 400 g risotto rice

1 cup / 250 ml dry white wine

2 cups / 500 ml vegetable broth (stock)

2/3 cup / 60 g freshly grated Parmesan cheese, plus additional for sprinkling

Method

Prep and cook time: 50 min

1 Cut off the tips from the asparagus and reserve. Thinly slice the stalks.

2 To cook the asparagus tips, bring ½ cup / 200 ml water, the sugar and a pinch of the salt to a boil in a saucepan. Drop in the asparagus tips and cook for about 5 minutes, until al dente. Remove from the pan, reserving the cooking liquid, and transfer to a colander under cold running water to stop the cooking; set aside.

3 Heat 1 tablespoon of the butter in a deep skillet until it foams, then add the asparagus slices and shallot and sauté until tender. Add the rice, stir well and sauté briefly. Mix the wine with the reserved asparagus water and vegetable broth (stock). Pour 2 ladlefuls of the mixture onto the rice and cook over a medium heat, stirring, until it has been absorbed. Continue to add the stock in this way, allowing the last ladleful to be absorbed before adding the next and stirring frequently.

4 When the rice is cooked but still slightly hard in the center, carefully stir in the asparagus tips, the remaining butter and the Parmesan cheese. Season to taste with salt and pepper. Serve on warmed plates sprinkled with coarsely grated Parmesan.

POTATO SALAD WITH SMOKED TROUT

Ingredients

1¾ lb / 800 g boiling potatoes

4 tbsp sour cream

2 tbsp mayonnaise

4–5 tbsp vegetable broth (broth)

White wine vinegar, to taste

2 scallions (spring onions), finely chopped

Salt, to taste

1 red onion, sliced

12 oz / 300 g smoked trout, flaked

1 handful fresh herbs, e. g. parsley or cress

2 tbsp capers

Method
Prep and cook time: 50 min

1 Place the potatoes in a steamer basket; set in a saucepan over 1 inch of boiling water. Cover and steam until tender, about 25 minutes. Drain and return to the hot pot to dry briefly, then peel and slice.

2 Mix the sour cream, mayonnaise, broth and vinegar in a large bowl; add the scallions and season to taste with salt. Add the potatoes and onion and toss gently to coat; spoon onto plates. Scatter the trout, herbs and capers over the salad and serve.

ASPARAGUS AND RICOTTA TART

Ingredients

For the pastry:

2²/₃ cups / 300 g all-purpose (plain) flour

²/₃ cup / 150 g butter, softened

1 egg

1 egg yolk

1 tbsp olive oil

1 pinch salt

For the filling:

1 lb (500 g) asparagus, trimmed; longer pieces halved

½ cup / 100 g ricotta cheese

3 eggs

1 cup / 100 g grated Parmesan cheese

Salt and freshly ground pepper, to taste

A few gratings of fresh nutmeg

Method

Prep and cook time: 1 h 40 min

1 Set the oven rack in the lower third of the oven. Preheat the oven to 400°F (200°C / Gas Mark 6). Grease an 8-inch / 22 cm square tart pan or round 9-inch / 24 cm quiche dish.

2 To make the pastry, combine the flour, butter, egg and egg yolk, ¹/₃ cup (100 ml) water, the oil and salt in a large bowl; work to a smooth dough. Form into a ball, wrap in foil or plastic wrap and chill for about 30 minutes.

3 Cook the asparagus in boiling salted water until bright green, about 5 minutes. Drain in a colander under cold running water to stop the cooking; set aside.

4 For the filling, mix together the ricotta, eggs and Parmesan cheese; season with salt, pepper and nutmeg.

5 Roll out the pastry to fit the dish and line the dish with the pastry. Top with the asparagus in an attractive pattern, then spread the ricotta mixture on top. Bake until lightly browned, about 45 minutes.

STUFFED TOMATOES

Ingredients

For the tomato sauce:

3 tsp olive oil

1/3 cup / 50 g finely chopped onion

2 cloves garlic, finely chopped

2 sprigs thyme

4 (7-oz / 200 g) beefsteak tomatoes, finely diced

1/2 cup / 100 g tomato concentrate (purée)

1–2 good pinches sugar

Salt and freshly ground white pepper,

For the tomatoes and stuffing:

4 (7-oz / 200 g) beefsteak tomatoes

1 tbsp. butter

1/3 cup / 50 g finely chopped onion

1 bay leaf

1 tsp fresh thyme leaves

1/2 cup / 100 g long-grain rice

1/4 cup / 30 g very thinly sliced carrot

1/3 cup / 30 g thinly sliced celery

1/3 cup / 30 g thinly sliced zucchini (courgette)

1/4 cup / 30 g frozen peas

2 tsp crème fraîche

2/3 cup / 75 g finely grated Gruyère cheese

1 tsp olive oil

Snipped chives, to garnish

Method

Prep and cook time: 1 h 20 min

1 Preheat the oven to 350°F (180°C / Gas Mark 4). Lightly grease a 1-quart / 1-liter baking dish.

2 For the tomato sauce, heat the oil in a skillet; add the onion, garlic and thyme and sauté until soft. Add the diced tomatoes and tomato concentrate (purée) and cook until the tomato is soft. Add 1 2/3 cups / 400 ml water and season with salt and pepper. Cook for a further 5 minutes or so. Check the seasoning and add more salt and the sugar if necessary. Purée the sauce in a blender and set aside.

3 For the tomatoes, cut off about the top third of each tomato to form a lid and set aside. Carefully hollow out the remainder of the tomatoes with a spoon and reserve the flesh.

4 For the stuffing, heat the butter in a skillet; add the onion, bay leaf and thyme and sauté until soft but not browned. Add the rice and sauté for 1 minute, then add 3/4 cup / 200 ml water, the carrot and 1 cup / 150 g of the tomato flesh. Season with salt and pepper. Bring to a boil, then reduce the heat and simmer for about 5 minutes, stirring occasionally. Add the celery and zucchini (courgette), then stir in the peas and simmer for about 15 minutes. Stir in the crème fraîche and grated cheese and season to taste.

5 Fill the hollowed-out tomatoes with the rice stuffing and put on the lids. Stand the stuffed tomatoes upright in the baking dish. Drizzle with olive oil and bake for about 20 minutes.

6 Shortly before serving, warm the tomato sauce. To serve, spoon a little of the tomato sauce onto warmed plates, put a stuffed tomato on each and garnish with snipped chives.

TRIPLE-DECKER PUMPERNICKEL SQUARES

Ingredients

1 bunch basil leaves

2½ cups / 600 g low-fat cream cheese, divided

Salt and freshly ground pepper, to taste

1 red bell pepper, diced

1 good pinch chili powder

1 tbsp tomato relish

1 tbsp ketchup

2 tbsp prepared horseradish

16 slices pumpernickel bread

Method

Prep and cook time: 30 min

1 Purée the basil leaves in a blender. Mix with 1 cup / 200 g of the cream cheese and season with salt and pepper; refrigerate.

2 Mix about ¾ cup / 150 g of the cream cheese with the diced bell pepper, chili powder, relish and ketchup; season with salt and pepper.

3 Mix the remaining cream cheese with the horseradish and season with salt and pepper.

4 Spread 4 slices of pumpernickel with each of the spreads and place one on top of the other. Top with the last 4 slices, wrap in plastic wrap and refrigerate. When well chilled, cut into quarters and arrange on a platter.

CHARD AND BACON TART

Ingredients

For the pastry:

1 small (5-oz / 150 g) baking potato, peeled

¾ oz / 20 g compressed fresh yeast

Scant ½ cup / 100 g lukewarm water

2 cups / 220 g all-purpose flour

Salt, to taste

A few gratings of fresh nutmeg

For the filling:

3 eggs

1 cup / 250 g crème fraîche

1 cup / 250 ml milk

4 oz / 100 g Roquefort cheese, mashed with a fork

4½ oz / 125 g Emmental cheese, grated

Salt and freshly ground pepper, to taste

1 tbsp vegetable oil

1 small eggplant, peeled and diced

1 onion, finely chopped

8 cups / 300 g chard leaves, trimmed and shredded (reserve a few leaves for garnish)

½ cup / 50 g shredded Gouda cheese

4 slices bacon

Method

Prep and and cook time: 1 h 10 min plus rising time: 1 h

1 Cook the potato in boiling salted water for about 15 minutes, until soft. Drain, let dry for a few minutes and push through a potato ricer while still hot.

2 Crumble the yeast into a small bowl and mix with the water, blending until smooth.

3 Combine the riced potato with the flour, yeast mixture, salt and nutmeg and knead to a smooth dough. Cover and put in a warm place to rise for 30 mins.

4 Meanwhile, whisk the eggs in a large bowl and stir in the crème fraîche and milk. Stir in the cheeses and season with salt and pepper.

5 Grease and flour a 10-inch (25 cm) tart pan with a removable bottom. Put the ball of pastry in the pan, then, using your fists and later, your fingertips, press the pastry out onto the base and sides of the pan. Cover and return to a warm place to rise an additional 30 minutes.

6 Heat the oil in a skillet; add the eggplant (aubergine) and onion and sauté until soft. Add the chard and cook until wilted. Pour off the liquid and spread the vegetables onto the tart pastry.

7 Spread the cheese mixture evenly over the vegetables, scatter with the Gouda cheese and lay the bacon slices on top. Put the tart onto the middle shelf of a cold oven, set the oven temperature to 400° F (200°C /Gas Mark 6) and bake for 35-40 minutes until browned, covering with foil if the tart browns too quickly. Serve garnished with the reserved chard leaves.

SPAGHETTI WITH SHRIMP AND COCONUT SAUCE

Ingredients

14 oz / 400 g spaghetti

1 leek

12 shrimp (or prawns), deveined and peeled apart from the tail segment

4 tbsp. oil

1 tsp. freshly grated ginger

2 cloves garlic, finely chopped

1 pinch curry powder

1 cup / 200 g finely chopped pineapple

scant ½ cup / 100 ml vegetable broth (stock)

scant ½ cup/ 100 ml coconut milk

Lemon juice

Sea salt

Shredded basil, to garnish

Method

Prep and cook time: 35 min

1 Cook the spaghetti in boiling, salted water until al dente.

2 Wash and trim the leek and cut into thin strips. Wash and dry the shrimp (or prawns).

3 Heat 2 tablespoons of the oil and sauté the leek with the garlic and ginger. Stir in the curry powder and pineapple and add the vegetable broth (stock) and coconut milk. Simmer for 1–2 minutes.

4 Meanwhile heat the rest of the oil and fry the shrimp for 1–2 minutes.

5 Drain the spaghetti, add to the sauce and toss to combine. Season with salt, add lemon juice to taste and serve into bowls. Add a few shrimp to each and serve sprinkled with basil.

SPINACH AND POTATO TORTILLA

Ingredients

14 oz / 400 g potatoes

2 tbsp vegetable oil

4 cups / 300 g baby spinach leaves

8 eggs

Salt and freshly ground pepper, to taste

Method

Prep and cook time: 35 min

1 Peel the potatoes and boil them in a pan of salted water. Slice them thinly once cooked.

2 Heat the oil in a large nonstick skillet and sauté the sliced potatoes until lightly browned.

3 Whisk the eggs in a bowl and season with salt and pepper. Pour over the potatoes and scatter with the spinach. Reduce the heat to medium-low, partially cover and cook for 10 minutes, or until the egg is set. Slide onto a plate and serve.

RICE SALAD WITH LENTILS

Ingredients

1 cup / 200 g wild rice

½ cup / 100 g long-grain rice

1 cup / 200 g brown lentils

3 tbsp olive oil

1 medium eggplant (aubergine), quartered and thinly sliced

1 red bell pepper, coarsely chopped

3 scallions (spring onions), coarsely chopped

Salt and freshly ground pepper, to taste

1 tbsp chopped fresh parsley

For the garlic dressing:

6 tbsp olive oil

Juice of 1 lemon

4 cloves garlic, chopped

1 pinch sugar

Salt and freshly ground pepper, to taste

Method

Prep and cook time: 1 h

1 Cook the wild and long-grain rice and lentils according to the package instructions; drain and keep warm.

2 Heat the oil in a large skillet over medium heat; add the eggplant (aubergine) and fry until golden brown, turning frequently. Add the bell pepper, reduce the heat, cover and cook until soft, adding 2–3 tablespoons water if necessary to prevent sticking. Stir in the scallions (spring onions) towards the end of cooking time. Gently stir in the cooked rices and lentils. Season to taste with salt and pepper. Let cool to room temperature, then stir in the parsley and adjust the seasoning if necessary.

3 To prepare the dressing, in a blender or mini food processor, pulse the oil, ¼ cup water, lemon juice, garlic, sugar, salt and pepper until smooth.

4 Spoon the rice salad into bowls and serve sprinkled with the garlic dressing.

ZUCCHINI FRITTATA

Ingredients

1 tsp butter, plus more for greasing the pan

2 zucchini (courgettes), trimmed and thinly sliced

2 large potatoes

6 eggs

½ bunch chives, snipped (reserve a few whole chives for garnish)

Salt and freshly ground pepper, to taste

Method

Prep and cook time: 45 min

1 Peel the potatoes and boil them in a pan of salted water. Slice them thinly once cooked.

2 Preheat the oven to 325˚ F (170°C / Gas Mark 3). Butter a 9-inch / 24 cm square springform pan.

3 Heat the butter in a skillet and fry the zucchini (courgettes) for 3 minutes. Arrange the sliced zucchini and potatoes in the pan in neat, alternating layers.

4 Beat the eggs with 2 tablespoons water, the snipped chives, salt and pepper; pour over the zucchini and potatoes. Shake gently to settle the egg, then cover and bake 30 minutes until the egg is set. Garnish with chives.

MINI SAVORY TARTS

Ingredients

Makes 12 mini tarts

1 cup / 200 g sun-dried tomatoes in oil

14 oz / 400 g thawed frozen puff pastry

3 mini mozzarella balls, thinly sliced

1 small eggplant (aubergine), thinly sliced

Salt and freshly ground pepper, to taste

4 tbsp pine nuts, toasted

Olive oil, as needed

1 handful arugula (rocket) leaves, trimmed, to garnish

Method

Prep and cook time: 40 min

1 Preheat the oven to 400°F (200°C / Gas Mark 6). Line a baking sheet with foil or parchment.

2 Finely chop the tomatoes, adding a little of the tomato oil, until they resemble a paste.

3 Roll out the puff pastry and cut out 12 circles using a 3-inch (8 cm) round cookie cutter. Spoon some of the tomato mixture on the top and season with salt and pepper. Top with a few slices of mozzarella, followed by eggplant (aubergine) slices. Sprinkle with a few pine nuts and drizzle lightly with olive oil.

4 Place tarts on the baking sheet and bake until lightly browned, about 15 minutes. Garnish with the arugula (rocket) leaves and serve immediately.

BEET HUMMUS WITH TORTILLA CHIPS

Ingredients

For the dip:

1½ cups / 300 g chickpeas

1 medium beet (beetroot), peeled and cut into ½-in / 2 cm dice

½ cup / 150 g tahini (sesame paste)

Juice of 1 lemon

2 tbsp olive oil

3 cloves garlic

1 pinch cumin

Salt, to taste

For the tortilla chips:

4 flour tortillas

2–3 tbsp olive oil

1 tbsp chopped fresh parsley

Coarse sea salt and freshly ground pepper, to taste

Method

Prep and cook time: 1 h 30 min plus soaking time: 12 h

1 Soak the chickpeas in water overnight.

2 Drain and place the chickpeas in a saucepan; add enough water to cover by 2 inches (5 cm). Bring to a boil, reduce the heat and simmer until the chickpeas are barely tender, about 40 minutes. Add the cubed beet (beetroot) and continue cooking until tender. Drain and rinse in a colander under cold running water.

3 Purée the chickpeas and beets, tahini, lemon juice, oil, garlic and cumin in a food processor or blender; season with salt. Transfer to a serving bowl, cover and chill for about 30 minutes.

4 Meanwhile, to prepare the tortilla chips, preheat the oven to 350°F (180°C / Gas Mark 4). Line a baking sheet with foil or parchment.

5 Cut the tortillas into triangles and place on the baking sheet. Brush with a little olive oil, sprinkle with the parsley and season with salt and pepper. Bake until golden brown, about 5 minutes. Let cool and serve with the hummus.

For a quicker version, use 3⅓ cups drained canned chickpeas and ½ cup drained canned beets; skip steps 1 and 2.

TAGLIATELLE WITH SHRIMPS AND LIMES

Ingredients

12 oz / 350 g shrimp (or prawns), peeled, deveined and ready to use

500 g tagliatelle pasta

5 tbsp olive oil

2 limes, zest and juice

1 tbsp butter

1 bunch fresh basil

salt & freshly milled pepper

lime wedges, to garnish

Method

Prep and cook time: 30 min

1 Rinse the shrimps under cold water, then pat dry.

2 Cook the tagliatelle pasta in boiling, salted water according to instructions on the packet, until al dente. In a bowl mix 4 tablespoons of olive oil with the lime juice and season with salt and pepper.

3 Fry the shrimps in 1 tablespoon of hot oil and 1 tablespoon of butter for about 2–3 minutes, stirring continually. Season with salt and pepper, place on the side and keep warm.

4 Drain the tagliatelle, keeping about ½ cup of the pasta water. Toss the tagliatelle with the lime and oil dressing, the pasta water, the shrimps, the lime zest and the basil leaves. Divide onto warmed plates, season with freshly milled pepper, garnish with lime wedges and serve.

BEAN AND CHEESE QUESADILLAS

Ingredients

1 tbsp vegetable oil

7 oz / 200 g bacon, diced

2 mild green chili peppers, sliced into rings

1 clove garlic, minced

1 tbsp tomato paste

1 (14 oz / 400 g) can red kidney beans, rinsed and drained

Salt, to taste

Cayenne pepper, to taste

4 flour tortillas

Scant 1 cup / 100 g shredded cheddar cheese

Method

Prep and cook time: 25 min

1 Preheat the oven to 400°F (200°C / Gas Mark 6). Line a baking sheet with foil or parchment.

2 Heat the oil in a skillet; add the bacon, chilies and garlic and fry until the bacon is cooked through. Stir in the tomato paste and 3–4 tablespoons water; add the beans and simmer, stirring, 2–3 minutes. Season with salt and cayenne.

3 Spread the bean mixture onto the tortillas, top with cheese and fold in half. Place on a cookie sheet lined with parchment paper and bake until golden brown, about 10 minutes.

MINESTRONE WITH PESTO

Ingredients

3 beefsteak tomatoes

4 boiling potatoes, peeled and diced

2 carrots, peeled, quartered lengthwise and thinly sliced

2 zucchini (courgettes), quartered lengthwise and thinly sliced

1 large onion, coarsely chopped

1 fennel bulb, trimmed and diced

1 cup / 150 g small soup pasta, such as ditalini or orzo

3 tbsp olive oil

1–2 tbsp prepared pesto (from a jar)

Salt and freshly ground pepper, to taste

Grated Parmesan cheese, to serve

Method

Prep and cook time: 1 h 10 min

1 Fill a large bowl with ice water. Bring a pan of water to a boil. Add the tomatoes and cook 5–10 seconds; quickly remove them with a slotted spoon to the ice water to cool. Drain the tomatoes and slip off the skins. Halve the tomatoes lengthwise and squeeze out the seeds, dice.

2 Return the water to a boil, then add the potatoes, carrots, zucchini (courgettes), onion, fennel, and tomatoes. Pour in the olive oil and return to the boil. Reduce the heat, cover and simmer until the vegetables are tender, 15–20 minutes. Add the pasta and cook until al dente. Season the soup with salt and pepper and ladle into soup bowls. Spoon a heaping teaspoon of pesto into each and serve immediately. Sprinkle with freshly grated Parmesan cheese.

EGG NOODLES
WITH CHICKEN
AND VEGETABLES

Ingredients

8 oz / 225 g dried egg noodles

4 tsp. sesame oil

4 oz / 100 g boneless, skinned chicken breasts, cut into fine shreds 2 inches / 5cm long

2½ tbsp oil

2 tsp light soy sauce

2 tsp dark soy sauce

1 tbsp rice wine or sherry

1 tsp salt

½ tsp freshly milled pepper

½ tsp sugar

3 tbsp finely chopped scallions (spring onions)

1 tbsp finely chopped garlic

2½ cup / 50 g finely shredded snow peas (mangetout)

1/3 cup / 50 g finely shredded cooked ham

For the marinade:

2 tsp light soy sauce

2 tsp rice wine, or dry sherry

1 tsp sesame oil

½ tsp salt & ½ tsp pepper

Method
Prep and cook time: 45 min

1 Cook the noodles in a large pan of boiling water for 3–5 minutes, then drain and refresh in cold water. Drain thoroughly, toss with 3 teaspoons of the sesame oil and set aside.

2 Combine the shredded chicken with all the marinade ingredients, mix well and marinate for about 10 minutes.

3 Heat a wok over a high heat. Add 1 tablespoon of the oil and when very hot and slightly smoking add the shredded chicken. Stir-fry for about 2 minutes and then transfer to a plate. Wipe the wok clean. Add the noodles, soy sauces, rice wine or sherry, salt, pepper, sugar and scallions (spring onions). Stir-fry for 2 minutes.

4 Reheat the wok until it is very hot, then add the remaining oil. When the oil is slightly smoking add the garlic and stir-fry for 10 seconds. Then add the snow peas (mangetout) and ham and stir-fry for about 1 minute.

5 Return the chicken and any juices to the noodle mixture. Stir-fry for 3–4 minutes, or until the chicken is cooked. Add the remaining sesame oil and give the mixture a few final stirs. Turn onto a warm platter and serve at once.

PENNE WITH TOMATOES AND GORGONZOLA

Ingredients

4½ cups / 500 g penne

9 oz / 250 g baby plum tomatoes

7 oz / 200 g tub crème fraîche

Salt & freshly milled pepper

7 oz / 200 g Gorgonzola cheese

Basil leaves, to garnish

Method

Prep and cook time: 35 min

1 Cook the penne in boiling, salted water until al dente, refresh in cold water and drain.

2 Wash and halve the tomatoes. Mix with the penne and crème fraîche and season with pepper and a little salt.

3 Put into a fireproof dish and crumble the Gorgonzola over the pasta and tomatoes. Put into a preheated oven (400°F / 200°C / Gas Mark 6)) for 10–15 minutes. Serve scattered with basil.

SPINACH AND EGG STRUDEL

Ingredients

2 tbsp butter

1 onion, finely chopped

1½ lb / 750 g spinach leaves, about 10 cups

Salt and freshly ground pepper, to taste

Ground nutmeg, to taste

2/3 cup / 150 g crème fraîche

1 egg

1 tbsp finely chopped parsley

1 (11-oz / 300 g) package frozen puff pastry, thawed

4 hard-cooked eggs, shelled and halved lengthwise

Milk, for brushing the pastry

Method

Prep and cook time: 1 h

1 Preheat the oven to 425°F (220°C /Gas Mark 7). Line a baking sheet with parchment or foil.

2 Melt the butter in a large skillet, add the onion and sauté until tender. Add the spinach and cook, stirring, until wilted; continue cooking gently for about 6 minutes. Season with salt, pepper and nutmeg; set aside and let cool.

3 Whisk together the crème fraîche and egg until smooth; add the parsley and stir into the spinach mixture.

4 Roll out the pastry onto a lightly floured surface. Spread the spinach filling on one third of the pastry, arrange the eggs on top, press in lightly and roll up the pastry. Brush with milk. Put the strudel on the baking sheet bake until golden brown, 30–35 minutes.

SPAGHETTI WITH HERBS AND PINE NUTS

Ingredients

14 oz / 400 g spaghetti

1/3 cup / 50 g pine nuts

2 tbsp / 30 g butter

1 clove garlic, finely chopped

1 dash white wine

1 good pinch lemon zest

2 oz / 50 g chopped mixed herbs (e.g. chives, chervil, basil)

Salt & freshly milled pepper

1½ oz / 40 g Pecorino cheese, freshly shaved

Chives, to garnish

Method

Prep and cook time: 30 min

1 Cook the spagehtti in boiling, salted water until al dente.

2 Toast the pine nuts in a dry skillet until golden brown. Take out and leave to cool.

3 Heat the butter and sauté the garlic, then deglaze with white wine and simmer until slightly reduced.

4 Drain the pasta, retaining a few tablespoonfuls of the water. Add the lemon zest, herbs and drained pasta to the garlic, toss to combine and add a few spoonfuls of the pasta water.

5 Season to taste with salt and pepper and serve scattered with Pecorino and chives.

CREAMY CORN CHOWDER

Ingredients

2 cans corn, drained weight 10 oz / 300 g

1 white onion, finely chopped

2 cloves garlic, finely chopped

1 red chili, deseeded and finely chopped

1 tbsp. olive oil

1 tsp. curcuma (turmeric)

2 small sprigs fresh rosemary

Juice of 1 lime

3 cups / 750 ml vegetable broth (stock)

½ cup / 100 g whipping cream

2 tomatoes, deseeded and diced

Salt & freshly milled pepper

Method

Prep and cook time: 25 min

1 Heat the olive oil in a skillet and sauté the onion, garlic and chili until soft. Add the curcuma (turmeric), a sprig of rosemary, and half of the corn and stir. Now pour in the lime juice, vegetable broth (stock) and cream. Cover with a lid and simmer for about 8 minutes.

2 Purée with a hand blender until smooth, then strain through a sieve into a saucepan. Bring to a boil. Add the remaining corn and the diced tomatoes.

3 Season to taste with salt and pepper. Garnish with a spring of rosemary and serve.

EGG AND TOMATO WRAP

Ingredients

2 scallions (spring onions), trimmed and cut into rings

1 large boiling (waxy) potato, cooked

4 eggs, hard boiled

2 tomatoes, cubed

1 red bell pepper, deseeded and cubed

¼ cup / 80 g salad cream or mayonnaise, more if required

1–2 tbsp. mustard, medium strength

1–2 tbsp. white wine vinegar

2–3 tbsp. sour cream

4–6 large wholewheat tortillas

Salt & freshly milled pepper

Method

Prep and cook time: 25 min

1 Dice the potato. Peel the eggs and cut into cubes. Mash the egg yolks and mix to a smooth paste together with the salad cream (or mayonnaise), mustard, white wine vinegar and sour cream. Season to taste with salt and pepper.

2 Add the tomatoes, bell pepper, potatoes, egg and scallions to the salad cream dressing and mix well. Spread the tomato and egg salad on top of the tortillas and roll up into a wrap. Cut in half, season with freshly milled pepper and serve in a bowl.

BEANS AND TOMATOES ON TOASTED BREAD

Ingredients

7 oz / 200 g canned white beans

1 small red onion, quartered and cut into short, thin strips

2 cloves garlic

1–2 tbsp vinegar balsamic

1–2 tbsp. lemon juice

Salt & freshly milled black pepper

3–4 tbsp. extra virgin olive oil

2 tsp. lemon zest

4 small bunches tomatoes on the vine

1½ cups / 25–50 g arugula (rocket)

8 slices rustic Italian white bread, or ciabatta

Method

Prep and cook time: 20 min

1 Rinse and drain the beans. Peel the garlic and finely chop 1 clove. Halve the other.

2 Mix the balsamic cream with the chopped garlic, lemon juice, salt, pepper, and olive oil, then mix with the lemon zest, onion, and beans.

3 Put the bread and the tomatoes into a hot oven (400°F / 200°C / Gas Mark 6) until the bread is toasted and the tomatoes are cooked. Rub the bread with the halved garlic clove. Pile spoonfuls of the vegetable mixture on each slice and top with arugula (rocket) and tomatoes. Serve at once.

LENTIL SOUP WITH HAM

Ingredients

1¼ cups / 250 g lentils

1 tbsp vegetable oil

⅓ cup / 50 g diced ham

About ½ pound / 250 g celery root (celeriac), peeled and finely diced

2 carrots, peeled and finely diced

1 onion, finely diced

2 bay leaves

1 small baking potato (about 4 oz / 100 g), peeled and diced

2 tbsp butter

2 tbsp sugar

¼ cup / 50 ml light cream

Salt and freshly ground pepper, to taste

White wine vinegar, to taste

Thyme, to garnish

Method

Prep and cook time: 1 h plus soaking time: 12 h

1 Soak the lentils overnight.

2 Heat the oil in a skillet and sauté the ham until lightly browned. Add the celery root (celeriac), carrots and onion and about 2 cups / 500 ml water. Stir in the lentils and bay leaves. Add the potato to the pan and simmer over a low heat for about 45 minutes, stirring occasionally and adding more water if necessary.

3 Melt the butter in a small skillet; add the sugar and heat, stirring, until caramelized. Stir into the lentil soup (take care-it may splatter). Remove the bay leaves. Stir in the cream, season with salt and pepper and season with vinegar. Serve, garnished with thyme.

CHICKEN SALAD PITAS

Ingredients

1 small grilled or roasted chicken

Scant 1 cup / 200 g mayonnaise

Scant ½ cup / 100 g sour cream

½ bunch parsley (about 1 oz / 25 g), chopped (reserve a few whole leaves for garnish)

1 red onion, coarsely chopped

1 tart green apple, cored, cut into eighths, and thinly sliced

1 clove garlic, minced

Salt and freshly ground pepper, to taste

4 pita breads, halved and split to make pockets

4–6 lettuce leaves

Method
Prep and cook time: 30 min

1 Skin the chicken, take the meat off the bone and shred or cut the meat into small pieces.

2 Combine in a bowl with the mayonnaise, sour cream, parsley, onion, apple and garlic; season with salt and pepper. Line the pita pockets with lettuce leaves, then stuff with the salad. Serve at once, garnished with parsley leaves.

BABA GHANOUSH WITH PITA

Ingredients

2¼ lb / 1 kg eggplant (aubergine)

1 small onion, coarsely chopped

2 tsp chopped fresh parsley

3–4 cloves garlic, chopped

About ½ cup / 100 g olive oil

3–6 tablespoons lemon juice

Salt and white pepper, to taste

4 pita breads

Method

Prep and cook time: 45 min

1 Preheat the grill (or preheat the oven to 400°F (200°C /Gas Mark 6). Pierce the eggplants (aubergines) in several places with a fork. Grill or bake until the skin blisters and wrinkles and the flesh is soft. Let cool, then halve lengthwise and scrape out the flesh, discarding the skin.

2 Roughly chop the eggplant flesh and purée in a blender or food processor with the onion, parsley and garlic. Stir in enough olive oil to produce a creamy paste. Season with salt and pepper and add lemon juice to taste. Spoon into four small bowls, cover and chill.

3 Warm the pita breads according to the package instructions: heat them in the oven or toast briefly on both sides in a dry skillet. Slice into strips and serve with the eggplant purée.

LEMON CHICKEN SOUP

Ingredients

4 stalks lemongrass, peeled and cut into thin strips lengthways

2 kaffir lime leaves, roughly chopped

2 oz / 50 g galangal, peeled and thinly sliced crossways

2 oz / 50 g ginger, peeled and thinly sliced crossways

1 red chili, deseeded and finely chopped

6 cups / 1¼ liter chicken broth (stock)

14 oz / 400 g chicken breast fillet

About 4 oz / 120 g chestnut mushrooms (brown button mushrooms), sliced

5-6 oz / 160 g shiitake mushrooms, sliced

4 tbsp lemon juice

4 tbsp fish sauce

Salt & freshly ground black pepper

Cilantro /coriander leaves

Method

Prep and cook time: 35 min

1 Put the lemongrass, kaffir lime leaves, galangal, ginger and chili into a pan with the chicken broth (stock), bring to a boil and simmer for 12 minutes.

2 Add the chicken breast and simmer for a further 5 minutes. Take the chicken breast out of the soup and cut into strips crossways.

3 Add the mushrooms to the broth with the chicken and cook very gently for 4 minutes. Add lemon juice, fish sauce, salt and pepper to taste. Sprinkle with cilantro (coriander) leaves before serving.

PANCAKES WITH SMOKED SALMON

Ingredients

For the pancakes:

Scant 2 cups / 200 g all-purpose (plain) flour

1²/3 cups / 400 ml milk

4 eggs

1 pinch salt

Butter, as needed for frying

For the filling:

About 1¼ cups / 300 g crème fraîche

1 tbsp lemon juice

Salt and freshly ground pepper, to taste

16 large slices smoked salmon

16 sage leaves (reserve additional leaves to garnish)

¹/3 cup / 50 g toasted pine nuts

¾ cup / 100 g shredded Emmental cheese

Method

Prep and cook time: 45 min plus standing time: 30 min

1 Preheat the oven to 300°F (150° C / Gas Mark 2) Line a baking sheet with foil or parchment.

2 In a large bowl, whisk together the flour, milk, and salt; beat in the eggs one at a time. Let the batter stand for 30 minutes. Add a little more milk if the batter is too thick.

3 Heat a little butter in a skillet over medium heat; pour batter to make small pancakes. Cook, turning once, until lightly browned on both sides; transfer to a plate and continue with the remaining batter to make about 16 pancakes.

4 In a small bowl, blend the crème fraîche and lemon juice until smooth and season with salt and pepper.

5 Spread each pancake with a dollop of crème fraîche mixture; top with a slice of salmon, a sage leaf, and a sprinkle of pine nuts; roll up. Sprinkle with the cheese and place on the baking sheet; bake until the cheese melts. Slice in half at an angle and serve on plates, garnished with sage leaves.

PROSCIUTTO AND CHICKEN WITH PEAS IN CREAM

Ingredients

4 skinless boneless chicken breasts

Salt and freshly ground pepper, to taste

8 sage leaves, plus additional leaves to garnish

4 large paper-thin slices prosciutto

12 oz / 350 g snow peas (mangetout)

Heaping 1 cup / 150 g frozen peas

1 scallion (spring onion), chopped

1 tbsp olive oil

½ cup / 125 ml meat, poultry or vegetable broth (stock)

¼ cup / 50 ml light cream

2 tbsp lemon juice

Method

Prep and cook time: 30 min

1 Season the chicken breasts with salt and pepper and place 2 sage leaves on each one. Wrap a slice of prosciutto around each breast and secure with toothpicks.

2 Bring a saucepan of salted water to a boil; add the snow peas (mangetout) and green peas and cook until bright green, about 5 minutes. Place in a colander under cold running water to stop the cooking; set aside.

3 Heat the oil in a skillet over medium heat; add the chicken and cook until browned on both sides and no longer pink in the center, about 10 minutes. Transfer to a plate and keep warm.

4 Return the skillet to the heat and stir in the broth (stock) and cream. Add the peas, snow peas and scallions (spring onions) and heat through. Add the lemon juice and season with salt and pepper. To serve, thickly slice the chicken breasts and serve with the peas and cream sauce. Garnish with sage leaves.

HUMMUS AND SPROUT PITAS

Ingredients

1–2 carrots, peeled and grated

1–2 tbsp vinegar

1-1½ cups / 100–150 g sprouted lentils or bean sprouts

6–8 tbsp prepared hummus

2–4 tbsp sour cream

Salt and freshly ground pepper, to taste

4 whole-grain pita breads, halved and split to make pockets

4 cups (10 oz) / 300 g) mixed salad greens

Method

Prep and cook time: 20 min

1 Mix the carrots in a bowl with the vinegar and sprouts.

2 In another bowl, blend the hummus with the sour cream until smooth and season with salt and pepper. Spread the hummus mixture on one side of each pita pocket, then fill with the carrots and sprouts. Season with a little more pepper, if desired. Serve on plates with salad.

CORNBREAD WITH BACON

Ingredients

1 tsp vegetable oil

12 oz / 350 g bacon, finely chopped

2 scallions (spring onions), finely chopped

½ cup / 120 g canned corn kernels, drained

½ tsp hot pepper flakes

2 cups / 350 g cornmeal

2⅓ cups / 350g all-purpose (plain) flour

1 tsp sugar

1 tsp baking powder

½ tsp baking soda

½ tsp salt

1½ cups / 375 ml buttermilk

2 eggs

2 tsp melted butter

1 tsp maple syrup

½ tsp freshly ground black pepper

Method

Prep and cook time: 1 h

1 Preheat the oven to 400°F (200° C / Gas Mark 6). Grease a loaf pan or line with parchment.

2 Heat the oil in a skillet and fry the bacon until crisp. Add the scallions (spring onions) and fry gently for about 5 minutes. Stir in the corn kernels and pepper flakes; remove from the heat and set aside.

3 In a large bowl, whisk together both flours with the sugar, baking powder, baking soda and salt. Add the buttermilk, eggs, cooled bacon mixture, melted butter, maple syrup and pepper and mix just until combined. Spread the batter into the pan and bake until a toothpick inserted in the center comes out clean, 30-40 minutes. Turn out of the pan; slice and serve warm.

MISO SOUP WITH VEGETABLES

Ingredients

2 tbsp miso

1 tbsp vegetable broth granules

1 small carrot, peeled and cut into matchsticks

¼ nori sheet, cut into thin strips

1 bunch radishes, trimmed and halved

½ tsp. ground ginger

Salt

Method

Prep and cook time: 15 min

1 Put the miso into a pan with 3 tablespoons water and heat until it dissolves. Add 4 cups / 1 liter water and the broth granules.

2 Add the radishes, carrots and ginger to the soup and simmer for about 4 minutes. Season to taste with salt. Divide the nori strips between 4 bowls, ladle the hot soup over them and serve.

SAVORY CARROT CAKE

Ingredients

For the cake:

4 eggs

Scant ½ cup / 100 ml olive oil

1 tsp salt

2 2/3 cups / 300 g all-purpose flour

Generous ½ cup / 50 g grated Parmesan cheese

½ cup / 50 g pine nuts

2 tbsp chopped fresh parsley

3 tsp baking powder

4 cups / 200 g finely grated carrots

Salt and freshly ground pepper, to taste

For the filling and garnish:

Generous ¾ cup / 200 g cream cheese

Scant ½ cup / 100 ml light cream, whipped

1 tsp horseradish

Salt and freshly ground pepper, to taste

Cooked baby carrots, to garnish

Watercress sprigs, to garnish

Method

Prep and cook time: 1 h 30 min

1 Preheat the oven to 350°F (180°C / Gas Mark 4). Grease a loaf pan.

2 Whisk the eggs with the oil and salt in a large bowl.

3 In a separate bowl, mix the flour, Parmesan cheese, pine nuts, parsley and baking powder; gradually stir into the egg mixture. Add the carrots and season with salt and pepper. Turn the batter into the pan, smooth the top and bake until a toothpick inserted into the center comes out clean, 50–60 minutes. Let cool completely.

4 Meanwhile, blend the cream cheese, cream, horseradish, salt and pepper in a bowl until smooth.

5 Split the cooled cake in half horizontally and spread the bottom half with the filling, reserving 4 tablespoons. Replace the top half of the cake, neatening the edges as needed.

6 To decorate, spoon the remaining filling into a pastry bag with a wide, round tip (or a plastic bag with one side tip cut off). Pipe the rest of the filling on top of the cake and decorate with baby carrots and cress.

SALMON IN PUFF PASTRY WITH YOGURT DIP

Ingredients

14 oz / 400 g cod fillet

2 tbsp dry white wine

2 tbsp lemon juice, divided

Salt and freshly ground pepper, to taste

2/3 cup / 150 ml light cream

Scant ½ cup / 100 g cream cheese

2 tbsp chopped fresh parsley

1 (11-oz / 300 g) package frozen puff pastry, thawed

About 1 lb / 500 g salmon fillet, skinned

1 egg yolk, beaten

2 tbsp sliced almonds

For the dip:

½ cucumber

Generous ¾ cup / 200 g plain yogurt

Scant ½ cup / 100 g sour cream

Lemon slices, to garnish

Parsley, to garnish

Method

Prep and cook time: 1 h 15 min

1 Prepare the cod stuffing: chop the cod fillet into chunks and combine in a bowl with the wine and 1 tablespoon of the lemon juice; season with salt and pepper. Put into the freezer for about 15 minutes.

2 Place the fish mixture, cream, cream cheese and parsley in a food processor or food mill and pulse until smooth. Return to the bowl, cover and chill.

3 Preheat the oven to 350°F (180° C / Gas Mark 4). Line a baking sheet with parchment or foil. Lay the pastry sheets on top of each other and roll out on a floured work surface to about 3 times the size of the salmon fillet. Place on the baking sheet.

4 Spread half of the cod stuffing on the middle third of the pastry. Place the salmon fillet on top, season with salt and pepper and spread with the rest of the stuffing. Brush the edges of the pastry with egg yolk and fold over the salmon. Brush the top with more egg yolk, sprinkle with the sliced almonds and bake until golden and puffy, 35–40 minutes.

5 Meanwhile prepare the yogurt dip: peel the cucumber, halve lengthwise and scrape out the seeds with a small spoon. Grate the flesh and squeeze it dry in a clean kitchen towel.

6 Combine the yogurt and sour cream with the remaining lemon juice and a little salt and pepper; stir in the grated cucumber.

7 To serve, slice the salmon pastry into 4 pieces, garnish with lemon slices and parsley and serve with the yogurt dip.

BEEF CARPACCIO BRUSCHETTA

Ingredients

8 oz / 225 g beef tenderloin, trimmed of fat

4 tbsp olive oil, divided

4 slices crusty wholewheat bread

1 clove garlic, peeled and halved

1 handful trimmed arugula (rocket) leaves, divided

1 avocado, pitted and thinly sliced

2 tbsp finely chopped walnuts

2/3 cup / 30 g freshly grated Parmesan cheese

1 tbsp walnut oil

3–4 tbsp lemon juice

Salt and freshly ground pepper, to taste

Method

Prep and cook time: 25 min plus 30 mins freezing

1 Preheat a broiler or grill. Pat the beef dry with a paper towel; wrap in plastic wrap and place in the freezer for about 30 minutes (to make it easier to slice).

2 Drizzle two tablespoons of the oil over the bread slices and toast on both sides in the toaster oven or broiler until golden brown. Rub the slices with the garlic.

3 Place half of the arugula (rocket) leaves on top of the toast and top with the avocado slices.

4 Take the beef out of the freezer and cut into very thin slices (the sliced beef can be pounded between layers of waxed paper until paper-thin, if desired). Layer the beef on top of the avocado slices. Sprinkle with the remaining arugula leaves, the chopped walnuts and Parmesan cheese.

5 Whisk the remaining olive oil with the walnut oil and lemon juice in a small bowl. Drizzle over the toasts. Season with salt and pepper and serve immediately.

MUSHROOM FLATBREAD

Ingredients

¾ oz / 20 g fresh yeast

1 pinch sugar

2½ cups / 250 g all-purpose (plain) flour

Salt

Butter, to grease the baking tray

For the topping:

5 oz / 150 g button mushrooms, sliced

2 shallots, sliced

Olive oil

Salt & freshly milled pepper

5 oz / 150 g goat cheese

½ bunch arugula (rocket) leaves

Method

Prep and cook time: 40 mins plus 45 mins rising time

1 For the dough, put the yeast into a large bowl with about ½ cup (125 ml) warm water and the sugar and mix smoothly. Then add the flour and salt and knead well until the dough is no longer sticky. Cover with a kitchen towel and put to rise in a warm place for 45 minutes, by which time it should have doubled in volume.

2 Preheat the oven to 425°F (220°C / Gas Mark 7). Knead the dough again (not too vigorously) on a floured work surface, then roll out thinly into 4 flatbreads and put on a greased cookie sheet.

3 Thinly slice the goat cheese and spread over the dough, then bake in the hot oven for about 15 minutes.

4 Heat 2 tablespoons olive oil and quickly sauté the mushrooms and shallots over a high heat. Season with salt and pepper, then remove from the heat.

5 Take the flatbread out of the oven, scatter evenly with the mushrooms, shallots and arugula (rocket) and served sprinkled with a little olive oil.

CHICKEN AND MANGO SALAD

Ingredients

1/3 cup /50 g hazelnuts, finely chopped

½ tsp hot red pepper (chilli) flakes

2 tbsp vegetable oil

1½ lb (600-700 g) skinless boneless chicken breasts

1 tbsp lemon juice

2 tbsp white wine vinegar

2 tbsp extra-virgin olive oil

Salt and freshly ground pepper, to taste

1 (5-oz) bag (150 g) spinach leaves

½ cucumber, thinly sliced

1 ripe mango, peeled and thinly sliced

Watermelon slices, for garnish

Method

1 Combine the chopped nuts with the pepper flakes and spread on a plate. One at a time, add the chicken breasts and lightly coat on all sides, pressing crumbs firmly to help them adhere.

2 Heat the vegetable oil in a skillet and fry the chicken until browned on all sides and cooked through, about 7 minutes. Transfer chicken to a plate and keep warm. Return the skillet to the heat and add the lemon juice, 2–3 tablespoons water, vinegar and olive oil; cook, stirring to loosen browned bits from the skillet, until slightly thickened. Season with salt and pepper.

3 Slice the chicken and arrange on plates with spinach, cucumber, and mango. Drizzle with the sauce and serve at once with watermelon slices.

SAVOY CABBAGE STEW WITH BEANS AND TOMATOES

Ingredients

4 tbsp. olive oil

1 large white onion, chopped

1 lb 6 oz/ 600 g savoy cabbage, roughly shredded

5 cups / 1¼ liters beef broth (stock)

2 bay leaves

½ bunch thyme

Salt & freshly milled pepper

12 oz / 350 g ripe tomatoes, halved

1 can white beans (about 12-14 oz / 350-400 g)

2 cloves garlic

1 tsp salt

Method

Prep and cook time: 45 min

1 Heat 2 tablespoons oil and sauté the onion until soft, then add the cabbage and sauté briefly.

2 Add the broth (stock), bay leaves and thyme. Season with salt and pepper, cover and cook over a medium heat for about 15 minutes.

3 Rinse the beans in a sieve and drain. Add the beans and tomatoes to the soup and simmer over a low heat for a further 15 minutes.

4 Peel and roughly chop the garlic, then crush in a mortar with 1 teaspoon salt, gradually working in the rest of the olive oil. Stir the garlic oil into the soup. Check the seasoning and serve hot.

ASPARAGUS AND POTATOES WITH CREAMY HOLLANDAISE SAUCE

Ingredients

1¾ lb / 800 g boiling potatoes

2 lb / 1 kg white asparagus, trimmed and peeled

2 lb / 1 kg green asparagus, trimmed

2 tbsp lemon juice

1 tsp salt

1 tsp butter

1 pinch sugar

Hollandaise sauce:

1 cup (2 sticks) / 250 g butter

2 egg yolks

4 tbsp dry white wine

2 tbsp lemon juice

Salt and freshly ground white pepper

In addition:

Chopped parsley, to garnish

Chives, to garnish

Method

1 Cook the potatoes in plenty of boiling salted water for about 30 minutes, until soft; drain and set aside. Keep warm.

2 Bring to a boil plenty of water with the lemon juice, salt, butter and sugar. Add the white asparagus and cook for about 18 minutes, adding the green asparagus after about 8 minutes. Lift out with a skimmer and drain.

3 For the hollandaise sauce, melt the butter and skim off the foam. Set a metal bowl over a saucepan of barely simmering water. Add the egg yolks and wine and beat until foamy. Then add the butter, first a few drops at a time, then in a thin stream, beating continually to produce a creamy sauce. Take care that the egg mixture does not curdle. Season to taste with lemon juice, salt and pepper.

4 Peel the potatoes, sprinkle with chopped parsley and serve with the asparagus and hollandaise sauce. Garnish the asparagus with a small bunch of chives.

BEEF ROULADES

Ingredients

1 small red bell pepper, cored and quartered

3 tbsp vegetable oil, divided

1 onion, chopped

4 beef roulades (thin 5-oz / 150 g) round steak pieces

Salt and freshly ground pepper, to taste

1 tbsp mustard

4 thin slices bacon

1 cup /250 ml beef or chicken broth (stock)

½ cup / 125 ml dry red wine

12–16 thin slices crisp-fried bacon, to garnish

Method

Prep and cook time: 1 h 20 min

1 Preheat the broiler (grill). Line a broiler pan with foil. Place the bell pepper pieces skin-side-up in the pan and broil until the skin blisters and blackens. Take out, cover with a damp cloth and let cool 10 minutes. Then pull off the skin.

2 Heat 1 tablespoon of the oil in a nonstick skillet; add the onion and sauté until translucent; set aside.

3 Season the meat with salt and pepper and spread mustard on one side of each slice. Then put a slice of bacon, a bell pepper piece and a little of the onion on each slice. Roll up from the narrow side and secure the end with a toothpick.

4 Heat the remaining oil in a large saucepan or Dutch oven over medium-high heat; add the roulades and brown on all sides. Add the broth (stock) and wine; cover and bring to just below a simmer. Reduce heat to low and cook at a bare simmer for about 45 minutes. Transfer the roulades to a plate and keep warm.

5 Return the saucepan to the heat and boil the sauce to reduce it slightly. Slice the roulades and serve with crisp fried bacon and sauce on the side.

FRITTATA WITH SMOKED SALMON AND MASCARPONE

Ingredients

Makes 2 frittatas

2 potatoes, peeled

2 tbsp vegetable oil

2 tbsp butter

1–2 mild red chili peppers, deseeded and finely diced

8–10 eggs

Salt and freshly ground pepper, to taste

12 oz / 300–400 g smoked salmon fillet, sliced into thin strips

3 scallions (spring onions), sliced into 2-inch / 5 cm strips

4–6 tbsp mascarpone

Method

Prep and cook time: 25 min

1 Cook the potatoes in a pan of boiling water. Drain and shred the cooked potatoes.

2 Add a tablespoon each of oil and butter to a medium nonstick skillet. Sauté the shredded potato and chilies for 1–2 minutes. Leave half of the mixture in the skillet and set aside the rest for the second frittata.

3 Beat the eggs with a little salt and pepper in a medium bowl and pour half of the egg mixture over the potatoes in the skillet. Scatter half of the salmon and scallions on top, stir gently, cover and cook over low heat for 8-10 minutes, until the eggs are set. Wrap the frittata in foil to keep it warm while you cook the second one.

4 Season with salt and pepper. Garnish with a few spoonfuls of mascarpone and serve.

RIBBON PASTA WITH CHEESE, TOMATO AND ASPARAGUS

Ingredients

1 lb / 500 g asparagus, trimmed

1 lb / 500 g fettuccine

2–3 sprigs rosemary

2 tbsp butter

1 small onion, thinly sliced

2 cloves garlic, thinly sliced

Scant ½ cup / 100 ml dry white wine

2/3 cup / 150 g sun-dried tomatoes in oil, drained and sliced into strips

7 oz / 200 g sheep's cheese, crumbled

Salt and pepper, to taste

Method

Prep and cook time: 25 min

1 Slice off the asparagus tips and thinly slice the stems along the diagonal.

2 Cook the pasta in plenty of boiling salted water according to the package instructions, adding the rosemary sprigs to the water. Add the asparagus pieces 5 minutes before the end of cooking time. Drain and keep warm.

3 Heat the butter in a deep skillet; add the onion and garlic and sauté until translucent. Add the wine and simmer, stirring to loosen browned bits from the skillet, for 2 minutes.

4 Add the drained pasta and toss to combine. Add the tomatoes and cheese and warm briefly. Season with salt and pepper and serve.

Published by Transatlantic Press

First published in 2010

Transatlantic Press
38 Copthorne Road, Croxley Green, Hertfordshire WD3 4AQ

© Transatlantic Press

Images and Recipes by StockFood © The Food Image Agency

Recipes selected by Jonnie Léger, StockFood

ISBN 978-1-907176-33-3

Printed in China